How to Read Your Husband Like a Book

Rajasekar KS

Leadstart
INKSTATE

ISBN 978-93-5458-252-3

First published in India 2021 by Leadstart Inkstate
A division of One Point Six Technologies Pvt Ltd

Sales Office:
Unit No.25/26, Building No.A/1,
Near Wadala RTO,
Wadala (East), Mumbai – 400037 India
Phone: +91 969933000
Email: info@leadstartcorp.com
www.leadstartcorp.com

Disclaimer: The views expressed in this book are those of the Author and do not pertain to be held by the Publisher.

Editor: Roona Ballachanda
Cover: R. Maharaja
Illustrations: Senthil B
Layouts: Kshitij Dhawale

This book is dedicated to all those happy couples who love, care, support and stand by each other and celebrate their differences, despite the eggs that life throws at them every day.

About the Author

Award-winning marketer, speaker and writer, Rajasekar KS has been happily married for 25 years. For the last eight years, he's been in the matchmaking industry with the Indian online matrimony leader, BharatMatrimony, where he spearheaded projects, including the launch of 'happymarriages.com, India's guide to a happy marriage', the 'Happy Marriage Workshops' attended by over 30,000 people and a 'Happy Couples' program that included over a 1500 interviews with newly married couples.

He has been recognised among India's Powerful Influencers 2020 by Adgully, listed in Top Content Professionals by Adobe & Paul Writer (2017 & 2018), recognised by Express Writers USA in the Top 100 Content Marketers, and ranked among the top 50 marketers in India by the World Marketing Congress. He speaks on culture, content marketing, social media and technology at various forums including Internet and Mobile Association of India, Exchange4Media, IFMR and social media summits. Occasionally, he has written for the online edition of Economic Times (Tech), Business World and Business Line.

Acknowledgements

Gratitude to my parents, KS Raju and Kanthamani, for their love and care.

Thanks to my artist Senthil B, who brought my thoughts to life.

Thanks to well-known author Dr P Raja, my English Literature Professor at college, who inspired me to write during my college days and after.

Thanks to my publisher who had faith in my book.

A special thanks to my wife, Kalpana, for the enduring love, care and support. And to my two cheerful daughters, Kritika & Sneha, for their love.

The two boxes inside a married man's head

Men are easy to understand, yes, but only after you've been married to them for 10 years. But in the intervening years, you will continue to lose hair thinking about why they forget your birthday, leave wet towels on the bed, don't notice your new hair style, watch TV when you talk to them… and more of such things.

The truth is they don't think too much. They have just two boxes in their head - "things to do now" and "Don't open this box". The first accounts for whatever they're doing at the moment - driving the car, on an office call, loading the washing machine or gazing at the neighbour.

The second one is all about weekend relaxation, the game or show tonight on TV, the upcoming meeting with old friends and their very male secrets and fantasies!

'How to Read Your Husband Like a Book' is my attempt to decode how men think and act in various situations. The intention is to help the newly married woman understand their "man" and enrich their relationship with this new understanding. You're sure to have "ahaa" moments as you flip through it.

To all the married men out there, I'm sorry for revealing what's on your mind. Afterall, someone's got to tell the truth!

The husband thinks that "work"
is what he does at office during
the weekdays
and that God created weekends
for him to rest and relax.

You may be able to wish and conjure up a dinosaur in your backyard but getting him to work on Saturdays and Sundays is IMPOSSIBLE.

The longer your question, the shorter his response.
The shorter your question, the longer his silence.

The husband loves to answer in monosyllables because he thinks it offers you less scope for an argument.

The husband likes to disproportionately blow up all the little things he does for you. He'll make you a cup of coffee and then act as if he made a three-course dinner for you.

His idea of making breakfast is to order on the food app and he seriously believes that he worked hard for it.

They are used to staying with
the boys' gang,
where it was okay to puke on
the dining table and drop the
smelly socks on the dog.

Husbands can see the mess in the house, but they don't let themselves feel it. Because they know that once they feel it, they will want to clear it.

The husband doesn't notice or process details.
He has the observation skills of a six-month-old baby.

**Men may not notice if you've had a new haircut,
so it's worse when you have just
a blister on your foot.**

He will ask you 50 times why you're silent but will not try to figure out why. Because he just wants to fix it, not understand what upset you. Your silence terrifies a man because he thinks he can figure out complex things like artificial intelligence and chess, but not your silence. Truth be said: the husband actually trembles inside when he faces a silent wife.

**The husband may be a rocket scientist,
but he can't figure out why you're silent.
You have to explain your reasons clearly.**

He conveniently forgets some things but certainly remembers all that his mother said during her visit last summer.

Men have such poor memory that sometimes they forget whom they married.

Eels are no match for them, and they will slip away before you can say, "Oh My God".

Husbands can change topics when faced with an uncomfortable situation. They turn silent and may even temporarily agree to a truce.

Men are men.
Their exaggerated sense of
importance has been drilled into
them by science books at school
and their mothers at home.

Men love it when their wives talk highly about them before others, even though they realise that their wife is exaggerating a bit.

Don't tell them that you read
this technique in this book.
To get him to work, all you have
to do is pretend that you can't
do it without him. Voila!
Like superman, he'll do it alone.

Tell him you can't do something because it's tough for you and he'll do it all by himself, with a smile.

Watch the husband in his eye
when he says this.
He rewinds to his school days
when he was confronted
by a six-foot bully.

If a husband says sorry,
it simply means he doesn't want an argument.

Your mother-in-law is always right, so thinks her son. Their love bonds better than anything Fevicol can do.

**If ever you want to see a man angry,
say a few things about his mother.**

Even when the credit card bills pile up to the roof, he'll behave as if the weather is cool in the Arabian desert summer.

Men like to pretend they're in control even when the brake and clutch is not working.

Husbands dislike shopping like
you do cockroaches,
because the activity involves
processing a lot of details
and his system crashes
every time he tries it.

He may not have 15 minutes to shop with you but will find five hours to watch TV or sleep with the kid sliding down his tummy.

Actually, the moment you're out
of your home, he just enjoys the
freedom and space,
until your return.

When you ask husbands to take care of the kids' homework, they usually end up giving them something to eat, and watch TV, while the kid flushes his paint box down the toilet.

The husband dreads
confrontation with the wife
about anything, not just
regarding why he lied to you
about the woman he met
yesterday at a party.
He also fears that when
your mom comes,
he'll lose your attention.

**Two things husbands don't like to hear:
"Can we talk for a few minutes?" and
"My mother is coming this weekend"**

The truth is while he loves you
to the moon and back,
he actually needs 10 hours away
from home, not necessarily you.

Going to work every day is the husband's way of saying "I love you dear."

You got to give this to them. But just be careful with what comes after that surprise gift!

The husband's way of showing they love you is to buy your favourite things without being asked.

If you ask him why he didn't
help you with something,
he'll say, "you didn't ask me.
I would've been happy to help".

**The husband is like the circus animal;
he'll easily learn any new tricks you teach him.
But he just won't try anything on his own 'cause he
fears that'll be the start of a deluge of work.**

The husband remembers his mother more after marriage. The reason being she never chided him for forgetting her birthday or the car keys, not doing household chores or leaving wet towels on the bed.

The way to get your husband to clean the kitchen is to persuade him to invite his mother next weekend.

A man's ego is as big as the Titanic. And it sinks fast when you make a comparison.

When you compare him to a colleague at work or your friend's husband, men feel emasculated and inadequate.

The husband many a time feels
something is wrong,
but the poor fellow just doesn't
know what is bothering you.
Unlike at the office, at home,
a husband thinks within a box,
not outside of it.

**When he massages your head or feet,
it means he has understood you're tired or upset,
but simply doesn't know why.**

The husband sometimes can
seek more attention than single
women at college.
But they feel ignored only when
they are bored,
or Netflix is down.

Husbands don't like it when you're on long calls with your friends 'cause they feel ignored.

He's as jealous as a school kid who sees a new toy in the hands of his classmate.

Husbands can't believe that they're not your first priority after a child.

Treat your man like a kindergarten teacher managing the kids in her class.
Just tell them what you want as specifically as you can.

Giving a man subtle clues is like talking Chinese to an Eskimo.

This is nothing to worry about and it will soon pass.

Husbands will drive to the airport at midnight to pick up the sister-in-law but feign office work when mother-in-law is coming home in the morning.

I'm not sure you've heard about the world's greatest escape artiste, Houdini, who'd escape from every possible difficult situation, even when handcuffed, put in a box and thrown into the sea. Every husband is a little Houdini.

When there's surplus money they'll want to manage the finances. When it's tough they'll volunteer to give you the honour.

I'm sure you understand this better than anyone else. They too need some attention, madam.

They love to steal a few glances at your pretty friends but get really upset when you casually enquire about his friend.

The husband is like the mother who, to keep the kids indoors, talks about the old man in the neighbourhood who kidnaps children who loiter outside home after dark.
Replace old man with yourself and the story is complete.

When your husband is angry with you, he'll make you a bad person when he's alone with the children.

You shouldn't for a moment confuse laziness with lack of interest to do things.

Husbands are not lazy.
Mind you they just don't like doing things at home.

The way he goes about choosing
a dress is to try on a shirt
or two at a store,
choose one and walk out as if he
designed it himself and exclaim:
Baby, my shopping is over!

**When you try on a new dress at a fashion store and he says, "you look terrific".
He actually means "Pack it and let's go for coffee soon. I'm tired of waiting."**

The husband switches off home
when he leaves to work.
At work, he forgets everything
about home and actually enjoys
it thoroughly.

When you call your husband and he says, "I was just thinking of you", it just means, "I had a lot of work today and forgot to call you".

Except sports or TV,
nothing can keep him attentive
for more than a few minutes.

If husbands seem bored during long conversations, it's not that they're uninterested... they just have very short attention spans

He wants to eat dinner so that he can soon get back to the TV.

**When your husband says,
"Can I help with dinner?",
he actually means, "why is it not ready yet?".**

Tomorrow never comes for him.
It's only today, nay only now!

**When your husband says,
"Can we talk about this tomorrow?" … he really
means "Don't bring up this topic ever again"**

He's telling you the truth because he knows you're talking, just that he doesn't know what you're saying.

When you suddenly stop talking and ask him, "Are you listening?" He'd say, "Of course, dear" when he actually wasn't listening.

Like the kings at war, they like
to deal with failures alone.
It's only when he succeeds does
he need someone to hold up his
big trumpet.

Husbands feel that a man has to deal with failures all by himself so when you remind him of it, he'll either go mad or he'll withdraw into a shell.

He believes that he's been sent into this world to save you from something, he's just trying to figure out from what.
And so are you.

Tell your husband that you feel safe with him and he'll do the impossible for you.

In the morning

In the evening

The husband is made
for simple things.
Go to work,
watch TV
and sleep.

The most complex thing a man can do correctly is drive the car. Though it has brakes, clutch, gear, accelerator and the horn in different places, he seems to manage it with ease. And even stuffs in a burger while driving.

You'll finally figure out that he's a boy who pretended to be a man when he won't pop his pills without you by his bedside.

When he's sick, he'll not allow you to leave his bedside, he'll seek all the attention.

When they're in a hurry,
they're like your grandma
without her glasses.
Watch out!

The rascal can demand attention like a kid and outlast your patience.

The umbilical cord is virtually intact in every husband. He thinks she understands him because she never questions him.

The only woman a man can understand is... you got it right, his mother.

They feel liberated when they
spend. God forbid if
a casino is near your home.

Men will do all the math when you want to buy something, but you will always find surprises when the credit card statement arrives.

They can't understand the fuss about him not knowing which class his child is in.
He thinks he's made for answering complex questions about rocket science, artificial intelligence or why the dog is refusing to eat his dinner today.

Men don't seem to remember too many details about their children, because birth was their goal.

The warrior thinks
the hunt is over. Period.

It might be surprising to know that men think that once you're married, you needn't compliment the lady for little things.

Unlike Monica in "Friends", the husband is at peace amidst mess at home.

**The wet towels on the bed, the smelly socks in the shoe cabinet and clothes strewn everywhere does not bother him at all.
Wait till his son starts doing it**

He can do only one thing at a time. If he's asked to do a second thing, his brain gets heated up like an old mobile and he'll forget his name after some time.

Unlike women, men don't really enjoy too many texts or calls from their spouses, while at work. They call it distraction.

In the beginning his complaint is you don't get along with his mom. In the end, it's like you hardly find time for him when his mom is around.

If you get along with his family, he'll be happy. If you get any further than that, he thinks you'll influence their decisions

Type everything onto his iPhone
and send him to the grocer,
or like the absent-minded
professor, he'll walk around the
market in circles not knowing
what to buy.

Your husband is most likely to be bad at shopping for grocery, in fact shopping for anything. It's just that he's not involved and will often end up either buying something you didn't ask for or forgetting to buy what you wanted.

Mr Know It All can't accept
that things have changed since
his childhood and that
he doesn't know the place
where he grew up.

**When you're out with your man, notice this.
He wouldn't want to ask directions.
He hates to accept he doesn't know the route.**

He thinks hair styling is all about getting a 10-minute nap at the salon while the hair dresser works on you.

Your husband can never figure out what all the excitement is, about getting your hair cut.

A wife who succeeds in getting a man who just got back from work to be attentive…. deserves an entry in the Guinness Book of World Records and a seat in the Oprah show.

**When he comes back from office, he'd actually love to go fishing for an hour, alone.
So, if you're not getting responses to your queries, you know he needs some silence.**

You'll sometimes wonder how's he's an Artificial Intelligence scientist at work when he can't figure out a simple clue at home.

He'd like you to come quickly to the point. Cues, hints and vague references won't work. Be direct.

Truth be said that when the protector can't protect, he feels vulnerable.

**When a man says, "I can't bear to see you cry",
don't construe that to mean he can feel your pain.
Truth is the scent of tears puts him off
and he feels inadequate because he's
not able to help you stop it.**

The husband always looks for
temporary truce
in any situation.

**If you hear him say "I'll do it"
when he's doing something else as you talk,
you be sure he's not doing it, because he wasn't
even listening to you in the first place.**

He understands the importance of allies who can be managed with mere lollipops versus his lady who he thinks won't be satisfied even with a Louis Vuitton bag.

You may be surprised to know that men always like to be in the good books of children.

Not with the occasional flowers and chocolates or movie dates; by not remembering birthdays or forgetting your child's school annual day.

Your husband can really surprise you at times.

For you, it's all in the details.
For him, it's good or not good.
No further distinctions possible.

If you ask him how a particular dress looks on you, don't be surprised if he doesn't say how it fits or if the colour adds to your personality.

"She will change you" is part of folklore, grandma's chit chat and men's talk at the bar. Hard to ignore the years of drilling into one's mind.

Many a man fears that that his wife might change him.

When men come back home, they want to look in the eye of their kids and feel they are heroes, even though they just returned from a day's work delivering pizzas in the neighbourhood.

Make a man a hero in the eyes of his children and he'll make you a queen in the eyes of the world.

He buries his mistakes faster than an ice cream melting on a hot summer afternoon.

He likes you to forget his mistakes and wishes you to pretend like nothing actually happened.

After marriage serious things
occupy his mind.
Will his favourite football team
win the trophy this year?
Will his boss return to office on
Tuesday or Thursday?
What will it be for dinner?

Before marriage, your man will talk silly things for long hours and very little after.

Often, your husband's behaviour has origins in his early life. Evolution, my dear.

To understand your husband, you must know his important family habits.

His mind has two boxes and he opens them one at a time.
Not more, not less.

**Your man will discuss only one thing at a time.
He'll not connect the disappearance
of some savings from his account to
his mother's visit last week.**

Even if you put a gun to his head, he can't decide what answer to give you!

When you ask for an opinion, a man could sometimes appear clueless. Don't misjudge him. He actually knows but he's afraid of your reaction.

He becomes dizzy when you explain what dress you wore, which handbag you matched, who else came to the party and who didn't, what was the conversation, that the food was awesome, Mrs X's kids got hurt by the pool, you didn't like the host's dress….

The husband is always confused when you explain every little detail of an event when he only asked you what time the party ended.

It makes you wonder sometimes if anything ever goes into his ears at all.

If you tell your man that you don't like the dog licking his face, he's most likely to kiss you immediately.

He simply can't figure out why the baby pees 10 times a day, wakes up just when he goes to sleep and refuses to drink the milk only when he tries feeding the baby.

Sometimes just when you need him to take care of the baby, he'll want to go to the restroom, attend an office call or rush to the car because he left something inside.

Every husband comes with a
manufacturing defect and no
instruction manual,
they will do something only
when asked to.

If you don't ask him for help, he'll be happy to let you do all the work.

He can open only one box in his
mind at a time.
So, when he opens the Friend's
box, his behaviour is limited to
the rules set in that box.

**Your man may behave differently when his friends
are around. Don't be flustered,
they have two sides to their personality.**

He's not meaning something else. Don't read meaning into what they say.
They just mean what they say.

When he says he wants to go to bed early, don't rush to the shower.

Wise old women will tell you
that you should never give the
husband a choice or chance.
If you do, you'll always regret it.

If you offer a choice, he will take the opposite of what you expect, with no malice intended.

You: Would you like to go to a movie today?

He: No. I'm watching a game tonight.

The husband is the soldier who takes commands and executes, never tries to think why a commander said so.

A husband acts and then thinks while you feel and then act.

Be very specific with your husband. If you're planning to change your car,
tell him that, instead of saying that your neighbour has got a new Mercedes and your boss's secretary rides a
Harley Davidson and your family is growing larger.

When you ramble along, he becomes like a three-year-old kid who's being lectured on Einstein's theory of relativity.

The husband likes to be in the
driver's seat all the time,
even if the car is
running off the cliff.

Your husband likes everyone including you to think he wears the pants at home, even though he lost it the first day after marriage.

The husband runs to office and walks to home.

The husband's office work never seems to end, and household chores never seem to begin.

Trumpets were made for men to use after marriage, especially when they have hardly anything to boast about in their day to day life.

A husband is one who after cleaning the home for 10 minutes acts as if he cooked, cleaned, laundered, mowed the lawns and made you exotic Brazilian coffee.

Men are boys in new clothes. They need to join the boys' gang, or they develop FOMO.

While being out with friends or travelling, your husband may act as if he's not enjoying himself... when in fact he's having the time of his life!

So, if you're asking him to do something and need to be out, be sure to call and remind him or when you return, you'll find him snoring and the child cutting open the sofa with the kitchen knife.

**Men can delay doing things at home for ever.
They just can't move themselves around after
they're back from work, especially on a weekend.**

Author's Note

I'm happily married for 25 years now. I truly believe that the wife-husband relationship is a beautiful one that everyone should be blessed with. The way a man thinks is completely different to a woman's inner mind. That's what makes a couple's relationship exciting, intriguing and sometimes challenging.

My book is a guide for married women to understand how the husband thinks and responds. I hope this book offers you a "new understanding" and helps improve your relationship with your partner.

I appreciate your time and effort in reading this book. Wish you happiness in everything you do.

If my book in any way left an impression on you, please let me know at positivemantra@gmail.com